Bub Is Stuck

By Sally Cowan

Sim, Pim and Bub looked for bugs in a stack of sticks.

"Stab the sticks with your bill, Bub!" said Sim.

Sim and Pim had lots of fun pecking in the sticks.

But they did not check on Bub!

Bub looked at a cricket.

It did a big hop
up some steps.

Bub ran up the steps
and into the shed.

Stop!

He got the cricket!

But then ... *Puff!*

Bub went stiff.

He got a big shock!

"Sim!" yelled Pim.

"Bub is not in the sticks!"

"Bub is not with me!"
Sim said from some
long stems.

Pim pecked at a crack.

"I will stab at the crack, too!"
said Sim.

When Bub got out, he still had the cricket in his bill!

I got stuck, but I got the big cricket!
Yum, yum!

CHECKING FOR MEANING

1. Why were Pim, Sim and Bub pecking in the sticks? *(Literal)*

2. Why did Bub get a big shock? *(Literal)*

3. What do you think Bub will do with the cricket now that he is out of the shed? *(Inferential)*

EXTENDING VOCABULARY

stack	What are two different meanings of this word? It can be a pile (a noun or naming word), or it can mean to pile things up in a heap (a verb or a doing word). Which meaning is used in this story?
stiff	How many sounds are in the word *stiff*? Which letter or letters make each of the sounds?
stems	What are *stems*? What can you often see at the top of a stem? What things do you know that have a stem?

MOVING BEYOND THE TEXT

1. Have you ever been locked in a room or in a shed because the door slammed shut? How did you get out?

2. Have you ever been caring for someone's pet when it got out or ran away? What did you do?

3. How do you think Pim and Sim felt when Bub got locked in the shed? Why?

4. Do you think Bub should have chased the cricket by himself? Should he have waited for Sim and Pim to be with him?

SPEED SOUNDS

| bl | gl | cr | fr | st |

PRACTICE WORDS

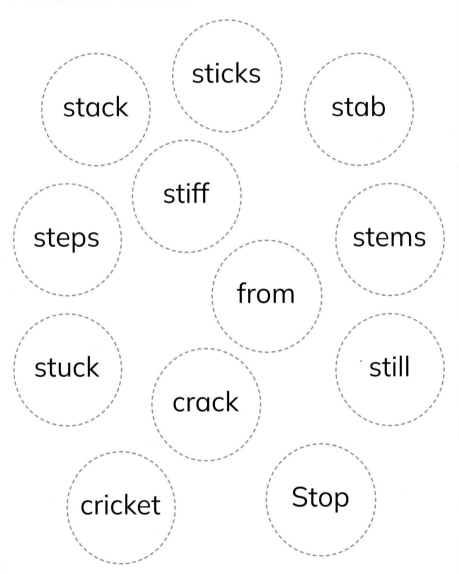

sticks

stack

stab

stiff

steps

stems

from

stuck

still

crack

cricket

Stop